Dahlia Inspirations

Life Lessons from the Dahlia Garden

Written & Photographed by
Rebecca McConnell

Dahlias bring beauty and wonder to our gardens, and to our lives. They offer us endless inspiration and opportunities to learn and grow. With their resilience, generosity and diversity, dahlias hold quiet wisdom for those willing to take time to observe and reflect.

This book is a collection of simple but empowering inspirations derived from growing dahlias - a reflection on how we can seed our own growth, embrace the ebb and flow of life, adapt to challenges and flourish in our own time and our own way.

May these pages inspire you to plant seeds of curiosity, nurture your dreams with care, and trust that in time, life, like our dahlias, will bloom in awe-inspiring ways.

Be Yourself

Dahlias express themselves in an astonishing range
of shapes, sizes, colours and forms. Each seed is the
culmination of near infinite genetic potential and will grow
a completely unique dahlia bloom - one of a kind.

From giant blousy dinnerplate decoratives, to tiny geometric
pompons and everything in between, we delight in the beauty
of their differences and embrace their individuality.

Dahlias are a joyful reminder to celebrate our own unique
strengths and grow and embrace who we are.

Cultivate Patience

Every gardener learns from dahlias the deep
satisfaction that arises from being patient.

Dahlias teach us patience as we wait for their first tender
shoots, and then again as we nurture those stems as
they develop over time into a strong robust plant.
We wait some more for each little bud to form, to fill
out, to colour and then to open out in all its glory.
We celebrate in its beauty, accept that it will fade, and wait again
while the plant gives bloom after bloom through the season and
then takes time to regroup and rest through a period of dormancy.

Dahlias teach us that good things are worth waiting for.

Grow Resilience

We endeavour to provide optimal conditions for our dahlia plants
to thrive. However, despite our best intentions, life happens and
unforeseen challenges sometimes arise. New pests, weather events
or unexpected disruptions or problems can thwart our efforts.

Despite setbacks, disappointments and failed expectations, the
key to flourishing is to accept how things are and to grow through
them, by being flexible and adaptable. We learn lessons and gain
knowledge through our failures and challenges and we don't give up.

Give Generously

When we give a nourishing environment to our dahlia plants, they
reward us by giving back tenfold. They deliver beautiful blooms that
go on for months. As the plants start to tire, we leave our blooms for
the bees and then collect seeds to create new and unique dahlias.
And to top it off, if we are fortunate, we discover under the soil a
full tuber clump that we can divide for extra plants the next year.

With the cornucopian abundance that dahlias give us, we
can likewise be generous and share the plentiful bounty
with others, and continue paying it forward.

The more we harvest our dahlias, the longer and better
they will grow, and we can perpetuate the generosity
and gift blooms, seed and tubers to others.

Celebrate Seasonality

Dahlias remind us to connect in with the ebb and flow of the seasons. To embrace the rise and fall of the cycles that play out through our lives. Like dahlias, we can pay attention to the natural seasons and flow with these. Dahlias remind us to take time to rest, to lie dormant at times so that we can spring forth with new energy when the time is right.

Taking time to really pay attention to what is happening around us, to mindfully notice our surroundings and to be grateful for the season of life that we are in right now, is truly a gift.

Seek Natural Balance

Dahlias draw energy from the sun, and send out their roots into the soil to form symbiotic relationships with the fungi and microbes below and draw in the moisture and nourishment deep down. When they are in balance with the environment around them, they thrive and perform at their optimal level.

They remind us to bask in the sunlight, drink deep of fresh water, nourish ourselves with healthy food and surround ourselves with the beauty of nature on a regular basis.

Treasure Each Moment

Each dahlia bloom is with us for only a few short days.
The bud opens, displays in all its glory and then fades.
Understanding and accepting the transient nature of life reminds
us to experience the joy in this very moment, and celebrate it.

True mindfulness is in paying attention. We can sit with our
humility, be grateful for what we have right now, to feel
the joy of being alive and accept things as they are.

Accept & Let Go

As each bloom comes to its natural end, we learn to let go
and accept that it is part of nature that the bud opens fully,
gives all of itself and then comes to the end of its season.
When we deadhead a spent bloom, harvest a stem, or take a seed
pod at the end of the season, we are making way for new buds
to form, and to share the beauty. We allow the plant to enter
dormancy so that the process can continue the next season.

Letting go allows for new growth and new beginnings.

About the Author

Rebecca McConnell is a flower farmer and dahlia breeder
at Serenade Farm on Tamborine Mountain, Australia.
She cultivates curiosity and nourishes her joy through
growing her beloved dahlias, surrounded by nature with her
husband Jon, and their two pups, Scout & Daisy.

When not in the garden, she plays the harp, knits jumpers,
reads frivolous fiction, listens to science podcasts and
loves to move freely and eat healthy food.

She is the author of a full length book, focused on Dahlia breeding, entitled
"Cultivating Curiosity - Growing Your Own Unique Dahlias from Seed".

All dahlias in this book were grown and photographed by Rebecca.

www.ingramcontent.com/pod-product-compliance
Lightning Source LLC
Chambersburg PA
CBHW041548260326
41914CB00016B/1582